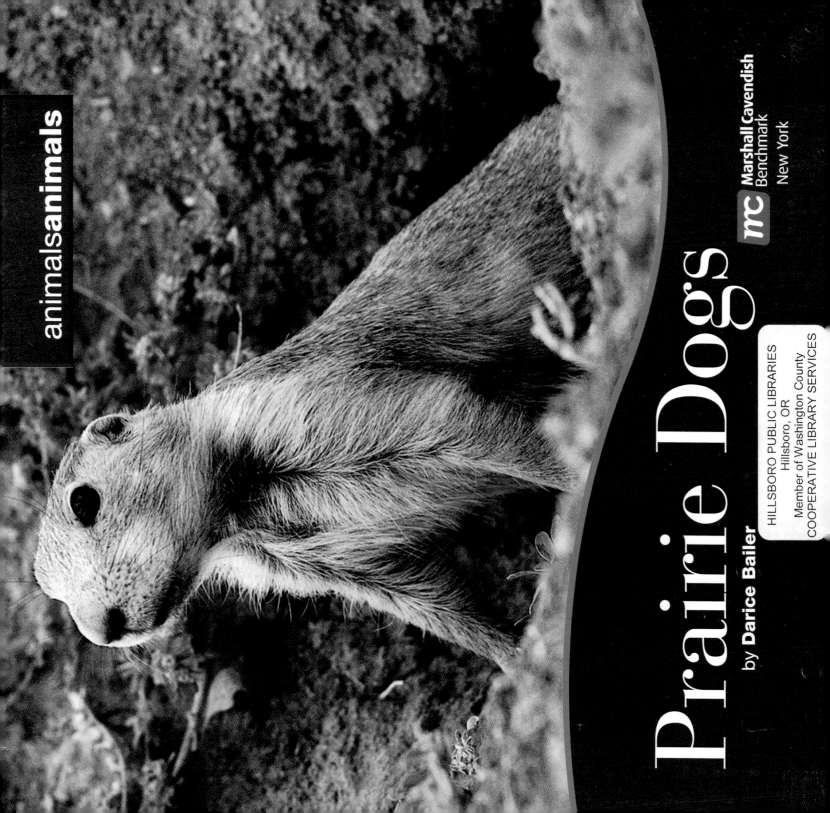

Prairie Dogs

by **Darice Bailer**

Marshall Cavendish
Benchmark
New York

Special thanks to Donald E. Moore III, associate director of animal care at the Smithsonian Institution's National Zoo, for his expert reading of this manuscript

Other Marshall Cavendish Offices:
Marshall Cavendish International (Asia) Private Limited, 1 New Industrial Road, Singapore 536196 • Marshall Cavendish International (Thailand) Co Ltd. 253 Asoke, 12th Flr, Sukhumvit 21 Road, Klongtoey Nua, Wattana, Bangkok 10110, Thailand • Marshall Cavendish (Malaysia) Sdn Bhd, Times Subang, Lot 46, Subang Hi-Tech Industrial Park, Batu Tiga, 40000 Shah Alam, Selangor Darul Ehsan, Malaysia

Marshall Cavendish is a trademark of Times Publishing Limited

All websites were available and accurate when this book was sent to press.

Library of Congress Cataloging-in-Publication Data

Bailer, Darice.
Prairie dogs / by Darice Bailer.
p. cm. — (Animals animals)
Includes index.
Summary: "Provides comprehensive information on the anatomy, special skills, habitats, and diet of prairie dogs"—Provided by publisher.
ISBN 978-0-7614-4876-1 (print)
ISBN 978-1-60870-618-1 (ebook)
1. Prairie dogs—Juvenile literature. 1. Title.
QL737.R68B335 2012
599.36'7—dc22
2010016033

Cover photo: Peter Arnold, Inc./Alamy

The photographs in this book are used by permission and through the courtesy of:
AP Images: Mike Stark, 35. Alamy: Richard Blunt, 7; John Van Decker, 8; blickwinkel, 9(t); Robert Shantz, 10(t & b); Tom Mackie, 15; Juniors Bildarchiv, 18, 20; Greg Force, 30; Manor Photography, 32. Corbis: W. Perry Conway, 12, 22, 24, 29, 38; George D. Lepp, 25; Kevin Schafer, 37. Getty Images: Jeff Foott, 1; Ronald Wittek, + David W. Hamilton, 26. Photo Researchers, Inc.: Kenneth W. Fink, 9(b); Laurie O'Keefe, 17.

Editor: Joy Bean
Publisher: Michelle Bisson
Art Director: Anahid Hamparian
Series Designer: Adam Mietlowski
Photo research by Joan Meisel

Printed in Malaysia (T)
1 3 5 6 4 2

Contents

1 Home on the Prairie

A gentle wind ripples waves of grass across a flat *prairie*. Suddenly, a tan furry head pops out of a *mound* of dirt and two shiny black eyes peer out at the grassy *plain*. It is a prairie dog, and the little black-tailed creature scouts around the entrance to its underground home, or *burrow*. This prairie dog will be outside the whole day, nibbling on plants so it can fatten up to survive the winter.

All the eating helps keep grass from growing too tall in the *grasslands*. Shorter plants help the prairie dogs see better and know when a *predator* is stalking them.

The scientific name for a prairie dog is *Cynomys*. The word comes from two Greek words, *kyn* for dog

A prairie dog scrambles to the top of its burrow, eager to begin its day.

and *mys* for mouse, and the name means dog-mouse. When the explorers Meriwether Lewis and William Clark first heard these animals barking while exploring the western frontier from 1804 to 1806, they called them "little toy dogs" or "wild dogs of the prairie."

Although prairie dogs live on prairies, they are not actually dogs. Prairie dogs belong to the *rodent* family, just as rats, mice, and beavers do. They all have two sharp front teeth on the top and bottom of their jaws. They evolved from ground squirrels about 2 or 3 million years ago. And though prairie dogs are related to ground squirrels, prairie dogs are larger and chubbier, with shorter ears, bigger teeth, and longer claws.

Prairie dogs are found only in North America. They live in the United States as far west as the Rocky Mountains and as far east as the Mississippi River. They also live in the area known as the Great Plains, which runs from southern Canada, south into northern Mexico. They live in this area because they can easily spot other animals that may be

Although prairie dogs are related to ground squirrels, they have shorter ears and longer claws for digging.

A black-tailed prairie dog.

Species Chart

◆ *Cynomys ludovicianus* is the black-tailed prairie dog, and it has white fur on its belly and is the most common. When scientists talk about prairie dogs, they usually mean black-tailed ones. Black-tailed prairie dogs are the kind that are usually in zoos.

A Mexican prairie dog.

◆ *Cynomys mexicanus* is the Mexican prairie dog that lives in a few areas of Mexico. There are so few of these animals that they are *endangered*, which means they are in danger of becoming extinct.

◆ *Leukos* is a Greek word that means white or light, and *Cynomys leucurus* is the white-tailed prairie dog. These animals have black spots above their eyes and live in Colorado, Wyoming, and Montana.

A white-tailed prairie dog.

9

A Gunnison's prairie dog.

◆ *Cynomys gunnisoni* is the Gunnison's prairie dog. It is the smallest of the five species and has a white tip on its brown or gray tail. Adults are about 12 inches (30 centimeters) long and weigh about 1 pound (454 grams).

◆ *Cynomys parvidens* is the Utah prairie dog. Although *Parvidens* comes from the Latin word *parvus* meaning small, Utah prairie dogs can be very big. They live in Utah and are light brown to reddish brown, with white tails and black patches above their eyes.

A Utah prairie dog.

after them, and there is plenty of grass for the prairie dogs to eat.

There are five *species* of prairie dogs. They all look alike, with brown or tan fur. However, some prairie dogs have black fur on the tips of their tails (the black-tailed and Mexican prairie dogs), and others have white (the white-tailed, Gunnison's, and Utah prairie dogs). Adult prairie dogs are only about 1 foot tall (30 cm) and weigh 1 to 3 pounds (454 to 1,362 g). The largest prairie dogs are about as big as rabbits.

Black-tailed and Mexican prairie dogs do not *hibernate* during the winter. However, white-tailed, Gunnison's, and Utah prairie dogs do hibernate in their burrows during the late fall and winter because temperatures are colder in the places where they live.

Prairie Dog Towns

2

Because they have so many predators, prairie dogs stick together for safety. They live in family groups called *coteries*, and black-tailed prairie dogs usually live with one adult male, two to three adult females, and a few *yearlings*. When male yearlings become adults, they move away. The females usually stay in the same coterie their whole lives, so there can be mothers, grandmothers, sisters, daughters, and aunts all in one burrow. Living together increases every-one's chances of survival.

Prairie dogs have an interesting way of greeting one another and finding out if nearby prairie dogs are family or not. They run up to each other and touch their noses together in what looks like a kiss. As they

A prairie dog family hovers atop its burrow, ready to dive for safety.

13

lightly touch their front teeth together, they are able to smell each other. Tasting and smelling help prairie dogs make sure that other dogs are not intruders to their area.

The family's burrows are more than just holes beneath the ground. Burrows have rooms as big as soccer balls, and they are all connected by tunnels. There are places for the prairie dogs to sleep together and for mothers to nurse their young. Some burrows are small, with only a few rooms linked by tunnels. Others are bigger and have many more rooms and up to 108 feet (33 meters) of tunnels. That is about as long as three school buses.

Burrows are important for safety. The family's burrows help protect the prairie dogs from predators, and they provide a safer place for mothers to give birth and nurse their babies. Burrows also protect the animals from very hot or very cold temperatures. On hot summer days, prairie dogs cool off inside the shade of their burrows.

The family lives with other prairie dog families in a number of burrows inside a neighborhood that is known as its *territory*. It is kind of like living with your family on a street filled with houses and being

able to go inside anyone's house whenever you want. You could sleep over at one house one night and another house the following night and no one would mind. That is the way it is with prairie dogs. They can dash into any burrow at any time of day to escape from an eagle or coyote and sleep wherever they want inside their territory. One territory might have thirty-five to fifty burrows. A bunch of coterie territories make up a prairie dog *colony*, or town. A large town might have hundreds of coteries, and their burrows might stretch for miles.

Burrows can have front and back holes, or entrances and exits, and the more entrances and exits

15

there are, the easier it is for prairie dogs to come and go and escape from their enemies. One entrance to the burrow often looks like a volcano with a rim that is 3 feet tall (1 m). That way, when rain floods the plain, the rim of the crater will be high enough to keep the burrow from flooding. High mounds of dirt also make excellent watchtowers so dogs can stand on top and look around the prairie for threatening animals. The opening to the burrow can be up to 12 inches (20 cm) wide. The tunnel narrows below.

The tunnel into a prairie dog burrow is usually about 6 to 10 feet deep (about 2 to 3 m). Halfway down the tunnel and below the entrance, there is a "listening room" where the animals can wait to see if an eagle, falcon, or coyote is outside. Prairie dogs can also turn around here or let another dog pass.

Some burrows have been in the family for generations. It is easier for prairie dogs to fix them up and add new rooms if they are needed instead of digging new ones. However, prairie dogs can also build new burrows, and they use their strong front

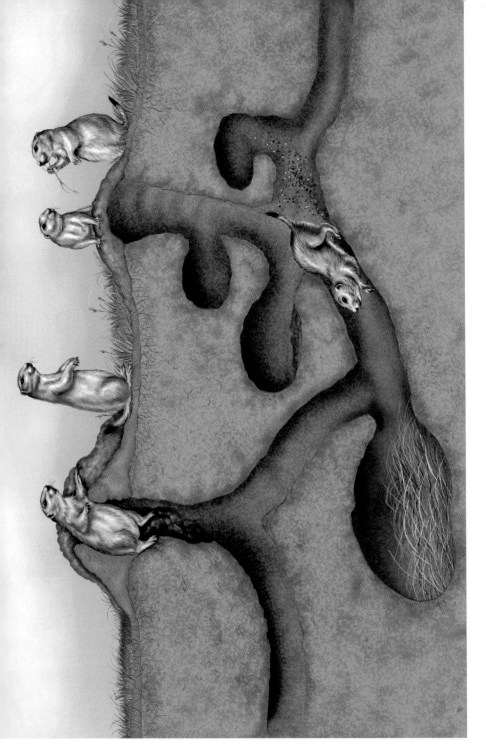

Prairie dog burrows have one or more entrances to their underground tunnels.

claws to dig and their noses, heads, and paws to pack the dirt. They even use their heads like jackhammers and pound down the dirt with their noses. A prairie dog's front teeth are very sharp and can easily bite through underground roots that might get in the animal's way while digging tunnels for its home.

17

Prairie dogs eat and look out for predators at the same time.

When the weather is good, prairie dogs spend most of their days outside the burrow, eating from sunrise to sunset. Their eyes see best during the daylight, and they eat while watching out for predators, rarely straying farther than 30 feet (9.1 m) from their burrows. They use their front paws to eat. Standing up on their hind legs, they scout the prairie for danger as they chew. They have large eyes set back on the sides of their heads, which help them to see a wide distance around them.

Prairie dogs eat mainly grass, but they will also eat other plants such as wildflowers, dandelions, weeds, and shrubs. Prairie dogs sometimes eat the whole plant, including the roots, stems, leaves, buds, flowers, and seeds. In the fall and winter, prairie dogs eat dried grass or whatever they can find. Because the Great Plains does not receive much rainfall, most of the time prairie dogs do not have puddles of water to drink from on the ground. They are able to get water from the juicy plants they eat.

3 Prairie Pups

When they are about two years old, black-tailed prairie dogs look for *mates*. They do this in the spring, when snow begins to melt. As green leaves begin to sprout in the still-cold ground, low chirping is heard across the prairie. The chirps sound like birds but with a *k* sound at the end: *chirk, chirk.* Those *chirks* are the mating calls of a male prairie dog. Mating season lasts two to three weeks, and most of the time a male will choose a female from his coterie to be his partner to have babies, called *pups.* The male then chases the female into the burrow, where the pair can be together safely.

The pregnant female chooses a room to raise her babies, called a *nursery.* Then she makes many trips outside, filling her mouth with bundles of grass that

This prairie dog is gathering bundles of dried grass for a warm nest.

21

These prairie dog pups are a week old and are still blind and furless.

have dried over the winter. A pregnant prairie dog may make more than two hundred trips outside the burrow to gather grass. She scurries underground and lays each mouthful in the nursery for a warm and cozy lining for her nest. She is pregnant for thirty-four or thirty-five days. Prairie dogs usually give birth to three or four pups at one time, but they can have as few as one or as many as eight at a time.

When they are born, the pups all have closed eyes and wrinkled red skin. The pups are a little more than 1 inch long (2.5 cm) and weigh about a half ounce (about 20 g). They are about the size and weight of an unshelled peanut and are blind at first. Their mother nurses them, licking them and keeping them warm beside her. When the pups are two to three weeks old, their mother leaves them alone for the entire day while she goes outside to eat. Then, at night, she returns to nurse. The young ones develop quickly. Their first coat of fur grows in about three weeks after they are born, and it is light and thin. Then, five weeks after they are born, the pups open their eyes and begin to crawl around the tunnels near their nest.

When they are about six weeks old, the pups are ready to explore life outside the burrow. The time when the young prairie dogs come outside is when they begin to stop nursing and feed themselves. The mothers are still busy inside taking care of everyone else's pups during the day. They use their front teeth to comb the pups' fur. They might roll around and *groom* the

Did You Know . . .

When pups come outside for the first time, they are on their own in what becomes one big day care center. All the pups get all mixed up. It seems as if mothers cannot tell which pups are theirs, and pups cannot figure out which one of the adult females is their mother! However, it is all one big, happy family.

23

A female prairie dog guards her two sleepy pups in her nest.

babies for a long time. Grooming helps prairie dogs rake off other dogs' dirt, fleas, lice, and ticks, so their fur stays clean and the animals do not get sick. Fleas spread *plague*, which is a disease that can easily kill a prairie dog.

When they are not eating, the pups chase one another, pounce, and wrestle. They grow stronger day by day and learn how to run from predators when

24

they get older. Sadly, about half the pups that are born each spring do not survive their first winter. They are eaten by predators or do not grow fat enough to survive. Heavier prairie dogs survive winter better than thin ones. They have more fat to help them endure hunger and cold.

If they do survive, most young males move out of the coterie when they are old enough to mate. Each one may scamper over to another coterie and challenge another dog to be the head male there. When the outsider faces the other male, the two will stare at each other, fluff up their tails, bark, and sometimes chase and fight each other. If the stray male loses the fight, he will have to go and challenge another male in another coterie for the right to live there.

Two black-tailed prairie dogs have fun playing in the dirt.

Prairie Dog Watch

4

Prairie dogs are never safe. There are animals that can attack them from the air, on the ground, or even in their own burrows. Therefore, prairie dogs are always on guard and working together with other family members to defend themselves. By living in groups, prairie dogs can look out for the others and warn their families when their enemies are nearby.

Most predators are too big to follow prairie dogs into their burrows. But *ferrets* can, and they are active at night when prairie dogs are sleeping. Once underground, ferrets can pounce on the sleepy animals and kill them with their sharp teeth. Badgers are also deadly. Though they are too pudgy to fit inside a burrow, they can dig up a prairie dog den with their

Badgers can dig up prairie dog burrows with their sharp claws.

27

paws. It might take the badger two or three hours to scoop out the little animals, but some badgers keep digging until they do.

Besides badgers, other animals such as coyotes, bobcats, and red and gray foxes also eat prairie dogs. Up in the sky, eagles and falcons will swoop down and grab prairie dogs with their sharp *talons*. A prairie dog can spend up to five hours a day looking for predators and barking when it sees them. These warning calls are critical for survival.

About half of the adults and yearlings bark when a dangerous animal creeps up on them, and usually because they have family or young ones nearby. The first prairie dog to see a predator will bark and warn the others. Prairie dogs might crouch inside the rim of their burrows and chirk, flicking their tails at the same time. Prairie dogs can stand up tall on their hind legs while barking, or sound an alarm on all fours. Their warning call can last just a second or two, but some prairie dogs chirk away for more than an hour. They can bark fast or slow, or in a high or low voice. The speed of their bark tells the

Did You Know . . .

A few nervous prairie dogs frequently bark an alarm, even if there is no danger. The other prairie dogs learn to ignore their calls. However, if prairie dogs hear two dogs barking, they run to the closest burrow mound. They know there is trouble.

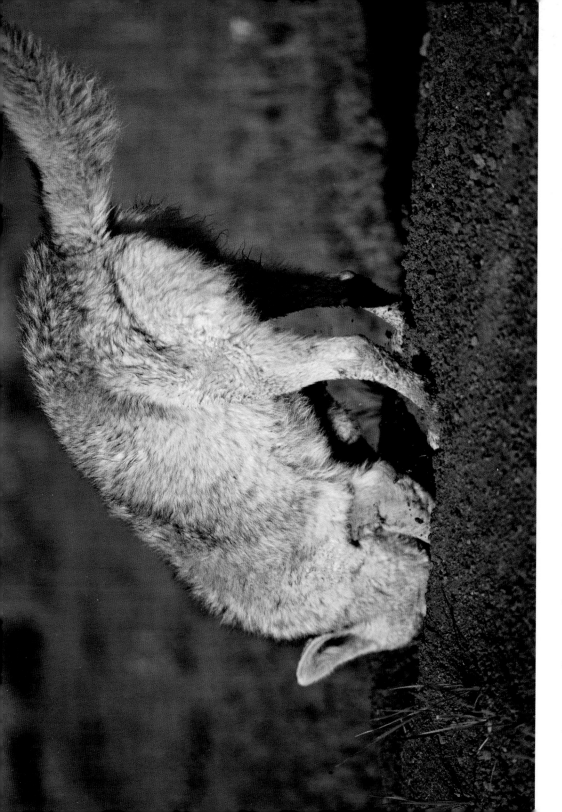

A coyote digs up a burrow and noses around for prairie dogs.

others how much danger they are in, or how quickly the danger is approaching, such as whether a falcon is flying slowly or a coyote is charging at them.

29

Danger is near: A prairie dog barks and warns the others.

Once prairie dogs start barking, others stop what they are doing and look around them. If they see the predator and it is dangerous, they run to their burrow mounds and perhaps join in the barking to make sure others understand the crisis. While chirking, they usually stay on top of their burrow mounds so they can quickly get back to eating when the enemy leaves the area.

Sometimes prairie dogs need to defend their territories against other prairie dogs. Males might visit other territories when looking for mates during mating season. Guarding the territory and fighting off intruders seems to wear down male prairie dogs. If they survive their first year, they usually live just one or two years more. If females manage to survive their first year, they live to be four or five years old. Sometimes they even live to be eight.

Little Friends on the Prairie

No one knows how many prairie dogs lived in North America two hundred years ago when pioneers and explorers first saw them, but experts guess there were probably more than 5 billion. In 1901, a government biologist estimated that there might be 400 million dogs living in one Texas prairie town alone! However, there are only 2 percent as many prairie dogs alive today as there were two hundred years ago. That means that for every one hundred prairie dogs living back then, only two are alive today.

The sad thing is that humans are the main reason prairie dogs are now so rare. Many ranchers and

The population of black-tailed prairie dogs seems to be growing.

farmers believe that prairie dogs are pests that eat the grass meant for their cows or bulls. Also, ranchers are afraid that their *cattle* will accidentally step into a prairie dog hole and break a leg, although that rarely happens.

As such, through the years, farmers, ranchers, and landowners have poisoned or shot these little animals with the help of government agencies. From 1912 to 1923, 31 million prairie dogs living in Colorado were poisoned. And, by 1932, Arizona had poisoned and killed all of its black-tailed prairie dogs. Today, more than 2 million prairie dogs are shot and killed each year for sport. Huge numbers of prairie dogs also disappeared when cities, highways, or shopping centers were built across the grasslands they call home. Plague also wiped out many prairie dogs.

Prairie dogs are now so rare that in the year 2000, the United States Fish and Wildlife Service (USFWS) thought they were likely to become extinct. However, the USFWS later changed its mind. There are actually more black-tailed prairie dogs living on more acres of land than experts previously thought, and their populations seem to be going up rather than down.

A prairie dog in Utah watches a round of golf from its burrow top.

That is good, because if prairie dogs do disappear, it will be a catastrophe for many living things. Most ecologists believe that prairie dogs are a *keystone species* in the North American grasslands, because more than 150 kinds of plants and animals depend on them. Prairie dog towns offer food and shelter to many creatures. They are at the bottom of the food chain and many animals in the grasslands depend on them for food. As prairie dogs die out, coyotes, bobcats, foxes, badgers, golden eagles, hawks, falcons, and other animals go hungry.

When prairie dog colonies were destroyed during the past century, ferrets no longer had their major source of food. By 1986, there were only eighteen black-footed ferrets left, and they are now one of the rarest mammals in North America.

A prairie dog burrow is a place for many different animals, birds, reptiles, spiders, and insects to escape the cold, heat, and predators on the grasslands. Toads, turtles, salamanders, and rattlesnakes may nest or hibernate in a prairie dog burrow. Rabbits, mice, and

Did You Know . . .

Prairie dogs are a symbol of the American West along with the American buffalo. In fact, the two animals have lived side by side for thousands of years. Buffalo like to eat the protein-rich grass in prairie dog colonies, and they also like to roll around in the dirt circling prairie dog burrows. Maybe it is to rub off some of their pesky fleas and lice.

Prairie dogs are very important to many grassland animals. This sign warns drivers to go slow in order to avoid hitting any prairie dogs.

PRAIRIE DOG CROSSING

A burrowing owl nests in an empty prairie dog home.

38

ants live in abandoned burrows, and black widow spiders sometimes build their webs inside.

A small brown spotted owl called the burrowing owl is another creature that sometimes uses empty prairie dog burrows for its nests. They will make empty burrows their home. Similar to prairie dogs, these owls will stand guard on their mounds to watch for predators. Also, when the owls hear prairie dogs bark at predators, it is a warning call for them as well, because badgers and coyotes eat burrowing owls, too.

Prairie dogs help keep long grass trimmed and soil fertile. They eat dead leaves, thereby helping new leaves grow. The new leaves have more protein for American buffalo, cows, and bulls. And when prairie dogs dig out their burrows and bring up deeper dirt to the surface, they are helping the soil. They mix sand, clay, and minerals in the soil so it becomes richer and healthier for plant growth and can hold more water. Plants absorb the minerals and use them to make proteins. And, when animals eat the plants, they are able to use the proteins in their bodies. Prairie dogs also fertilize plants and soil with their waste droppings. Grazing animals, such as cows, like to eat these more nutritious plants.

Now you can see that prairie dogs are some of the most important animals in the grasslands. Though small in number, they have a huge impact on the plant and animal world around them. Countless wildlife depend on them for survival. People are starting to understand that these animals are some of the most important creatures on Earth. Letting prairie dogs die out now would be a great tragedy.

Glossary

burrows—The underground homes that prairie dogs dig for shelter.

cattle—Cows, steers, bulls, and oxen that are often raised for food.

chirk—The sound of a prairie dog's bark or mating call.

colony—Groups of prairie dogs living in the same area.

coterie—A prairie dog family that lives together in a burrow and defends its territory.

endangered—An animal that is in danger of extinction.

ferrets—Skinny animals with tan bodies and black fur around their eyes that make them look like little bandits.

grasslands—Wide, open spaces of flat and grassy land.

groom—To clean dirt and tiny insects from an animal's fur.

hibernate—To fall into a long, deep sleep so an animal can survive the cold winter when food is hard to find.

keystone species—An animal or species that is very important to its environment because many plants and animals depend on it for survival.

mates—Male or female partners who produce young.

mound—A hill or pile of dirt around a burrow hole.

nursery—A room in a prairie dog burrow where a mother can take care of her babies.

plague—A very serious bacterial disease that is spread by flea bites and kills many prairie dogs.

plain—A large, flat, and usually treeless land.

prairie—A large open area that is flat and covered by grass and has very few trees. The word *prairie* means meadow in French.

predators—Animals that hunt other animals for food.

pups—Young prairie dogs.

rodents—Warm-blooded animals with two sharp front teeth that are good for cutting and biting.

species—A group of animals that share common traits and characteristics.

talons—The sharp claws of a bird of prey.

territory—The area that prairie dogs defend so they can eat, sleep, and raise their pups.

yearlings—Young prairie dogs that are at least nine months old but less than twenty-one months old.

Find Out More

Books

Aronin, Miriam. *The Prairie Dog's Town: A Perfect Hideaway.* New York: Bearport Publishing, 2009.

Hoogland, John L. *Conservation of the Black-Tailed Prairie Dog: Saving North America's Western Grasslands.* Washington, D.C.: Island Press, 2005.

Jackson, Tom. *Prairie Dogs.* Danbury, CT: Grolier, 2008.

Markle, Sandra. *Prairie Dogs.* Minneapolis, MN: Lerner Publications Company, 2008.

Websites

Defenders of Wildlife: Prairie Dogs
www.defenders.org/wildlife_and_habitat/
wildlife/prairie_dog_black-tailed.php

Desert USA: Prairie Dogs
www.desertusa.com/dec96/du_pdogs.html

National Geographic: Prairie Dogs
http://animals.nationalgeographic.com/ani-
mals/mammals/prairie-dog

Prairie Dog Coalition
www.prairiedogcoalition.org/children-and-
education.php

Prairie Dog Lover's Burrow
www.prairiedoglover.com/forkids.htm

San Diego Zoo: Mammals: Prairie Dog
www.sandiegozoo.org/animalbytes/
t-prairie_dog.html

Index

Page numbers for illustrations are in **boldface**.

About the Author

Darice Bailer has been a teacher and freelance journalist for many years, contributing to *The New York Times*, *Greenwich Time*, and *The Hartford Courant*. She is also the author of many books for young readers and has received the Parents' Choice Gold Award and a Connecticut Press Club award for her books. She lives in Connecticut with her family.